Face-to-Face WOLVES

What's Inside?

Roaming the Forests

Wolves are wild dogs that live in lonely forests and on snowy plains. They are fierce-looking creatures with thick fur and sharp teeth, but they are shy. In fact, wolves will try to keep away from you. There are two main types of wolves — gray wolves and red wolves.

The coats of gray wolves come in different shades.

A baby wolf is called a pup. It looks like a tiny version of its parents!

A red wolf is the rarest of all the wolves.

[A]rctic wolf is a gray wolf with a snowy white fur coat.

3

Gray Wolf

A gray wolf is an expert hunter.
In summer, it usually sleeps during
the day, but it heads off at night
to look for moose or deer to eat.
In winter, it may hunt in the
daytime, too. Gray wolves live
in the northern part of the world,
far from towns and cities. Despite
their name, gray wolves can be
gray, brown, black, or even white.

Q **Do wolves have a wake-up call?**

A Yes, and it's a loud one! When it's time
to set off on a hunt, one early-rising wolf
howls as loudly as it can to tell the others
to get ready for the trip.

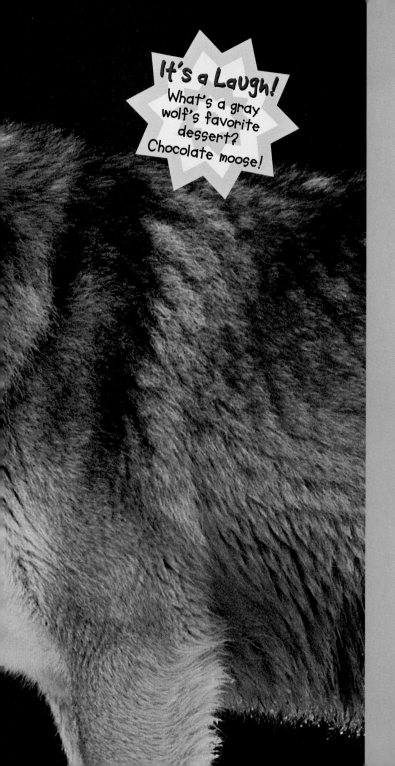

It's a Laugh!
What's a gray wolf's favorite dessert? Chocolate moose!

❋ A gray wolf has 42 ferocious teeth. The four longest teeth are called fangs and are perfect for gripping food. Each fang is longer than your finger!

❋ Young gray wolves play games to keep alert. One wolf sneaks up behind another, then suddenly it leaps in a zigzag pattern toward its pal!

❋ Gray wolves appear to love rolling in smelly meat and rotten fruit! After their relaxing bath, other wolves seem to think they smell wonderful.

Leader of the Pack

Wolves live together in family groups, called packs. Gray wolf packs have from 3 to 30 wolves, including a mom and dad, aunts, uncles, brothers, and sisters. A pack lives on a large area of land, called a territory. If strange wolves come near, the pack quickly chases them away.

▼ We're in Charge

A mother and father wolf lead the pack. They are called alpha wolves. They make all the decisions and keep the family in order.

▼ Singing Practice

Wolves howl to communicate with one another. Often, a pack gathers for a family singalong. Scientists believe the wolves howl together to make them feel part of one gang.

Can You Believe It?

For most of the year, arctic wolves change location every day! They roam around looking for prey and they sleep in a different place each night.

No slacking off at the back!

▼ Body Language

Wolves talk to one another using their faces and bodies. The young wolf lying on the ground has misbehaved. Now she is saying, "Whatever you say goes."

WOW!

A wolf pack's territory can be huge. One pack may roam around an area larger than New York City!

Arctic Wolf

An arctic wolf roams around an icy area in the far north of the world called the Arctic. This magnificent animal has a thick, white, furry coat and huge paws. It travels great distances across the snowy plains, hunting for large reindeer called caribou, which are its favorite food.

Q **How does an arctic wolf keep warm?**

A An arctic wolf snuggles down in a deep pile of snow to stay out of the cold wind. It tucks in its paws and curls its body into a tight ball.

DO NOT DISTURB

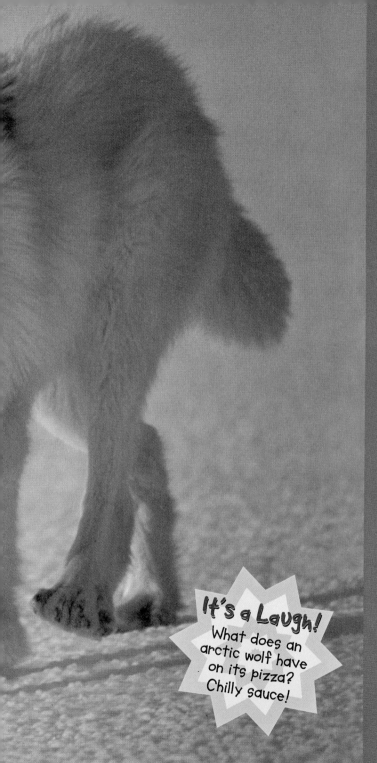

✻ An arctic wolf's paws are just like snowshoes! They help to stop the wolf from sinking into the snow and leave behind prints almost twice as big as your hand!

✻ In summer, most of the snow in the Arctic melts. An arctic wolf's coat changes color from white to grayish brown, to blend in with the background.

✻ Arctic wolves are excellent at fishing. Sometimes they wade into icy streams, then catch tasty salmon with their sharp teeth.

On the Prowl

When a wolf is out and about, it has all kinds of ways of finding food and keeping out of trouble. A wolf's supersharp hearing and amazing sense of smell warn of nearby enemies such as bears. If the wolf is lucky, it may find a juicy snack!

▶ Follow Your Nose

A wolf can sniff out things that you can't smell at all. Once a wolf picks up the trail of another animal, such as a deer, it can follow the smell for miles.

Can You Believe It?

To us, one howling wolf sounds just like another one, but actually each animal has its own special call. When a wolf loses its friends, it howls until it finds them — for hours and hours and hours!

▲ Acrobatic Ears

A wolf can turn its ears sideways, backward, and forward to follow the sounds of other animals on the move. Now, you try that!

▼ Keep Your Distance

When a wolf meets an enemy, the wolf snarls and bares its sharp teeth to show it is not scared. Only a brave creature hangs around to see if the wolf will bite!

Red Wolf

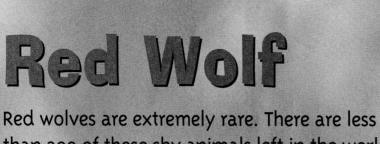

Red wolves are extremely rare. There are less than 300 of these shy animals left in the world. The only ones left in the wild live in the U.S.A. Red wolves are smaller than gray wolves and they live in smaller packs. Sometimes, a red wolf pack is made up of only a mother and a father wolf and their young.

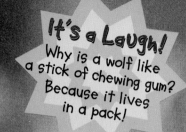

✻ Red wolves are very friendly to one another. When they meet, they often touch noses. Maybe it's their way of kissing!

✻ Red wolves used to roam all over the southeastern U.S.A. Today, they only run wild in special wildlife parks in North Carolina and Tennessee.

NORTH CAROLINA

TENNESSEE

Q Why are there so few red wolves?

A In the past, people cut down forests where the red wolves lived, so the wolves lost their homes. People also shot the wolves because they were afraid of them. But today, the wolves are protected.

SAVE THE RED WOLF

✻ Red wolves munch mainly on small animals such as rabbits and mice. Now and then, they may catch a deer, which makes a mouthwatering feast!

Mmm, tasty!

13

What's for Dinner?

Wolves love to feast on large animals, such as moose. But how does a wolf catch an animal bigger and stronger than itself? It works in a team with four or five other wolves. First, the team treks through the forest. Watch what happens next....

Can You Believe It?

Although wolves are experts at tracking down large animals, they don't always manage to catch their prey. Eight out of 10 times, their dinner escapes!

Oh no! There goes another one!

1 I Smell Dinner!

As soon as the leader smells a moose in the distance, it stops and sniffs the air. Other wolves do the same. Then they set off toward the moose.

2 Don't Make a Sound

When the wolves are close to their prey, they creep toward it quietly. They try not to let the moose know they are nearby.

3 Time to Pounce

Usually, the moose spots the wolves and starts to run. Quick as a flash, the wolves give chase. If they are lucky, they catch up and bring the moose to the ground.

WOW!
A wolf can eat up to 22 pounds (10 kilograms) of meat in one meal. That's the same as 88 hamburgers!

Wolf Pup

In spring or early summer, a mother wolf gives birth to as many as six babies, called pups. The tiny pups are blind at first and hide away with their mother in a warm underground den or cave. After a couple of weeks, their eyes open and soon the young animals grow strong enough to explore the outside world.

When a wolf pup is born, it weighs about 1 pound (0.5 kilograms). That's about the same as a jar of honey!

Young pups may move several times to find a safer home. The mother picks up each pup with her teeth, then takes them one by one to the new den.

Wolf pups have their own baby-sitters! When the mother and father wolf go hunting, another pack member stays behind to look after the young.

Q What is a wolf pup's favorite meal?

A A young wolf pup feasts on mushy meat. The pup's mother swallows the meat, then coughs it up. The meat is now soft enough for the young pup to eat. Yuck!

Mmm, my favorite!

Time to Move On

At the age of nine months, a young wolf can look after itself and might decide it's time to leave the pack. The lone wolf starts a tough life on its own. In time, however, it will find a new home, new friends, and may start a pack of its own.

▶ Keep Away!

Wolves in packs are unfriendly to strangers. If a lone wolf comes too close to a pack, the gang chases away the outsider.

▶ Pack Fight

A young wolf may fight with one of the pack leaders. If the young wolf wins, the old leader will leave and the young wolf will become the leader. But if the young wolf loses, it must leave the pack.

WOW!

When food is hard to find, a lone wolf can go up to two weeks without eating anything!

▲ A Hard Life

A lone wolf cannot catch big animals on its own. Instead, it feeds on mice, rabbits, and even young sheep from nearby farms. It also looks for scraps left behind by nearby packs.

3 In other old stories, people turned into hairy beasts called werewolves, which were half human and half wolf.

Aaagh! I need help!

4 Even though these stories were not true, wolves were unpopular. People shot at wolves that came near their homes and drove the animals far away.

Down with the wolves!

They don't like us, do they?

5 But eventually people had a change of heart. Wolves had become so rare, they were hardly ever seen in the wild.

What's that Dad?

It's a wolf. They used to live around here.

6 Special parks were set up to protect the wolves and give them the space to roam. Now, there is no need for wolves to be scared of people or for people to be scared of wolves!

Humans are funny!

That's right, son! Let's go for a run!

21

Puzzle Time

Here are a few puzzles to try. You can look back in the book to help you find the answers.

True or False?

How much do you know about wolves? Answer these true-or-false questions to find out.

1 Wolves like to bathe in rotten fruit. Hint: Go to page 5.

2 Arctic wolves never eat fish. Hint: Go to page 9.

3 Red wolves greet each other by smiling at each other. Hint: Go to page 13.

4 Wolves baby-sit one another's pups. Hint: Go to page 17.

Hide-and-Seek

How many wolves can you see hiding in this picture?

Snapshot

Look at the faces of these wolves. Can you tell which type of wolf each one is? Hint: Go to pages 2 and 3.

1

2

3

Index

Created by act-two for Scholastic Inc.
Copyright © act-two, 2001.
All rights reserved. Published by Scholastic Inc.
SCHOLASTIC and associated logos are trademarks
and/or registered trademarks of Scholastic Inc.

Main illustrations: Alan Male
Cartoon illustrations: Simon Clare
except for pp. 20–21 Geo Parkin, p. 23 Alan Rowe
Consultant: Barbara Taylor
Photographs: cover FLPA/T. Fitzharris/Minden Pictures, pp. 4–5
NHPA/Manfred Danegger, pp. 8–9 BBC Natural History Unit/Lynn
Stone, pp. 12–13 FLPA/Mark Newman, pp. 16–17 OSF/Daniel J. Cox

ISBN 0-439-31712-6

12 11 10 9 8 7 6 5 4 3 2 1   1 2 3 4 5 6/0

Printed in the U.S.A.

First Scholastic printing, November 2001